ARMOND
DALTON
PUBLISHERS
INC.

Alvin A. Arens

D. Dewey Ward

Carol J. Borsum

COMPUTERIZED ACCOUNTING

using QUICKBOOKS PRO 2018

FIFTH EDITION

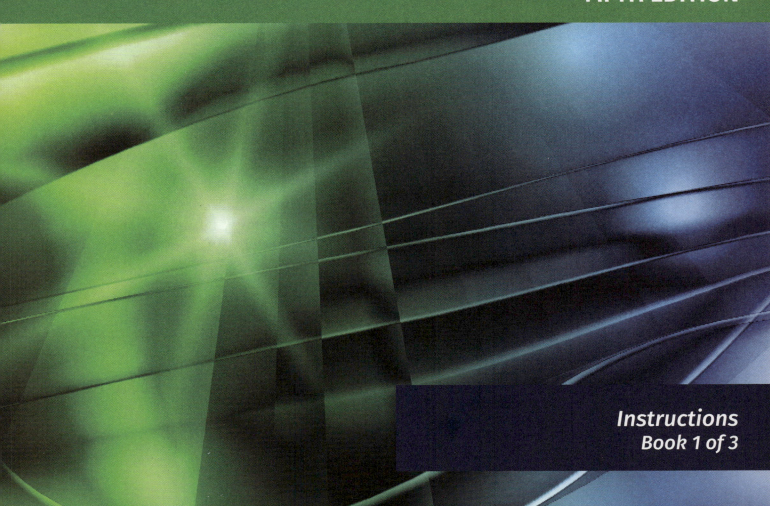

Instructions
Book 1 of 3

Images used on the front cover and throughout this book were obtained under license from Shutterstock.com.

TABLE OF CONTENTS

Introduction   1

Familiarization   2

(continued on the following page)

Familiarization *(continued)*

2

Overview of Maintenance, Processing Information, and Internal Controls

3